Windsor Castle

by Grace Hansen

Abdo Kids Jumbo is an Imprint of Abdo Kids
abdobooks.com

abdobooks.com

Published by Abdo Kids, a division of ABDO, P.O. Box 398166, Minneapolis, Minnesota 55439.

Printed in the United States of America, North Mankato, Minnesota.

052021

092021

Photo Credits: Alamy, Getty Images, iStock, Shutterstock PREMIER

Production Contributors: Teddy Borth, Jennie Forsberg, Grace Hansen
Design Contributors: Candice Keimig, Pakou Moua

Library of Congress Control Number: 2020947646

Publisher's Cataloging-in-Publication Data

Names: Hansen, Grace, author.

Title: Windsor castle / by Grace Hansen

Description: Minneapolis, Minnesota : Abdo Kids, 2022 | Series: Famous castles | Includes online resources and index.

Identifiers: ISBN 9781098207328 (lib. bdg.) | ISBN 9781098208165 (ebook) | ISBN 9781098208585 (Read-to-Me ebook)

Subjects: LCSH: Windsor Great Park (England)--Juvenile literature. | Castles--Juvenile literature. | Architecture--Juvenile literature.

Classification: DDC 728.81--dc23

Table of Contents

A Protective and Private Castle

In 1070, King William I began construction on Windsor Castle. Windsor was part of a chain of castles. This chain formed a protective ring around London, England.

King William I
England
London
Europe

Windsor Castle was **private** but close to London. It was also near popular hunting land. Because of this, **royals** liked to stay there. Henry I had built a place to live within Windsor by 1110.

King Henry I

Changes Over the Years

Late in the 1100s, Henry II built **royal** apartments at Windsor. Henry III worked to make the apartments more **luxurious**. Beginning in the 1350s, King Edward III began to turn the castle into a **Gothic**-style palace.

King Henry II
King Henry III
King Edward III

In 1475, Edward IV began work on St. George's Chapel. The beautiful **Gothic**-style chapel took 50 years to complete. It has held many **royal** funerals and weddings.

King Edward IV

Queen Elizabeth I took the throne in 1558. She also took over a castle in need of repair. Along with the repairs, the queen built a long gallery for indoor walks. Today, the gallery is part of the **Royal** Library.

Queen Elizabeth I

In 1685, King Charles II completed work on the Long Walk. But this project was not for strolls. It was to add **drama**. The paved walkway sits between 2.5 miles (4 km) of elm trees.

King Charles II

Between 1820 and 1830, King George IV made big changes at Windsor. He raised the Round Tower by 30 feet (9 m). He built other large spaces and added grand entrances.

King George IV

English rulers of the 20th century, including Edward VII and George V, worked to **modernize** Windsor. Queen Elizabeth II was crowned in 1952. She **restored** the castle and made it her weekend home.

King George V
Queen Elizabeth II

Windsor Castle Today

Today, Windsor is still a **royal** household. The castle hosts leaders from around the world. It is also a popular tourist destination.

THE
LOWER
WARD
SHOP
THE LOWER WARD SHOP

More Facts

- Many royals are buried in St. George's Chapel, including Edward IV, Henry VI, and Queen Mary.

- The Great Kitchen at Windsor was built between 1357 and 1377. It has served 32 rulers in its time.

- A fire in 1992 greatly damaged Windsor Castle. St. George's Hall was one area that had to be rebuilt. The hall was originally built for knights. Today, it can seat hundreds of people for important meals.

Glossary

drama – having an exciting or out of the ordinary effect.

Gothic – of or relating to the style of architecture characterized by its pointed arches and ribbed vaults.

luxurious – expensive, fancy, and giving great comfort.

modernize – to make modern or bring up to date.

private – quiet and away from much of the general public.

restore – to return to an earlier or normal condition.

royal – of or having to do with a king or queen, or any members of their family.

Index